Diary *of a*

Weeping Widow

From Mourning to Morning

TONI SINGLETON ADAMS ED.S

DIARY OF A WEEPING WIDOW
FROM MOURNING TO MORNING

Scripture quotations marked KJV are from the Holy Bible, King James Version (Authorized Version). First published in 1611. Quoted from the KJV Classic Reference Bible, Copyright © 1983 by The Zondervan Corporation.

iUniverse books may be ordered through booksellers or by contacting:

iUniverse
1663 Liberty Drive
Bloomington, IN 47403
www.iuniverse.com
1-800-Authors (1-800-288-4677)

Because of the dynamic nature of the Internet, any web addresses or links contained in this book may have changed since publication and may no longer be valid. The views expressed in this work are solely those of the author and do not necessarily reflect the views of the publisher, and the publisher hereby disclaims any responsibility for them.

Any people depicted in stock imagery provided by Getty Images are models, and such images are being used for illustrative purposes only. Certain stock imagery © Getty Images.

ISBN: 978-1-5320-5229-3 (sc)
ISBN: 978-1-5320-5228-6 (e)

Library of Congress Control Number: 2018912132

Print information available on the last page.

iUniverse rev. date: 12/13/2018

AN EXPLANATION OF THE FRONT COVER ILLUSTRATION

The picture on the front of this book has three pivotal items mentioned in Maya Angelou's "On the Pulse of the Morning." This poem was recited during former president William J. Clinton's inauguration in 1993. The poem's overall theme is a message of inclusion within our country. In the poem, she repeatedly speaks of the rock, the river, and the tree. The rock symbolizes strength. The river is symbolic of life. The tree planted by the water is the premise of the inspirational gospel song "I Shall Not be Moved," which is often sung in African American congregations. The origin of this message stems from Psalm 1:3. The tree is a reminder that nothing shall shake our faith, for it is planted and deeply rooted. To weather the storm of grief, depression, and loss, we need to speak life, have strength to overcome, and hold on to faith.

In Memory of My Loving Husband

Ben was a devoted husband and a caring father. He served as a pastor, community activist, and friend to many. He mentored many youth during his thirty-two years in education. He had a heart of compassion for anyone in need. In 2014, Ben represented Seminole County Public Schools as the School-Related Employee of the Year. In less than three months after receiving this honor, he went home to be with the Lord.

CONTENTS

Introduction xi

Prologue xiii

Part 1: The Struggles of Being a Widow

The Challenge of Getting to Know Me 1

    Hello 2

    You Want the Truth or the Lie? 4

    Invisible 6

    The New Me 8

    Who Is My Neighbor? 10

    To Work or Not to Work, That Is

    the Question 12

A New Role 15

    Where Are You? 16

    Nightly Runs 18

    Single or Widowed 20

    I Am Not the Only Widow 22

    It Didn't Happen to You 24

    Widow to Widow 26

    What Now? 28

It's Mourning Time 29

    4:55 A.M. 32

    Triggers 34

    Do the Dead Talk? 36

I Didn't Forget It's Our Anniversary 38

Surviving versus Living 40

Crazy or Grieving? 44

Truth Is Stranger than Fiction 46

Battle Scars 48

Rejected Stone 51

Now What? 54

You Couldn't Wait? 56

Negative People Got to Go! 58

Victimized 60

The Island of Misfit Toys 62

In-Laws, Ex-Laws, and Outlaws 64

These Three 66

Part 2: The Business Side of Being a Widow

Dotting Every I and Crossing Every T 71

A Widow's Might 74

Checklist 76

Smart Investments 78

Show Me the Money 80

Record It or Write It Down 82

A Widow's Vocabulary Words 84

Part 3: The Miraculous Power of God's Healing

Metamorphosis 89

The ABCs of Widowhood 92

Pruning 96

There Are Two Kinds of People in the World ... 98

Is It the Devil or God? 100

Thank You, Lord 102

Shall We Dance? 104

How Much Do I Owe? 108

Memory Lane 110

Saying Farewell 113

My Wedding Rings 114

His Stuff...116

Good Night 118

The Bedroom 120

Living the Good Life 121

Forgive Me—I Was Wrong........................... 124

Oh, Happy Day 126

Grandma 128

My People.. 130

My Christmas Present, 2015 136

The Power of Love 138

Spiritual Awakening.................................141

The Healing Place.................................... 144

New Hope 146

The Lord Is My Shepherd......................... 150

Levels of Christianity 152

My Last Will and Testament...................... 154

At the End of the Day................................ 156

Mourning to Morning............................... 158

Summary: A Christian's Responsibility................. 159

Resources for Widows 163

Special Days for Widows.......................... 165

Facts about Widows 167

Scriptural Mentions of Widows 169

Statistics about Widows............................171

Famous Young Widows/Widowers 173
Ways to Help Widows..175
Seven Ways Churches Can Show They Care
about Widows... 177
References...179

INTRODUCTION

This three-year journal is dedicated to widows, their families, and their friends. It is my desire that widows and their loved ones gain a greater insight regarding the world of widowhood. Simultaneously, I wish for everyone to know and understand my story. It is not necessarily every widow's story. Grief is unique as our DNA. No two widows are identical.

This book represents my personal journey, which may or may not have commonalities with other widows. This book is dedicated to my late husband. Ben—or honey—was the love of my life since I was a seventeen-year-old girl! Ben was my prom, debutante, and grad night date. We grew together and met the challenges of infertility, balancing family versus the ministry, and rearing children.

This journal is dedicated to our children, Willow and April. You have been there through times of destruction and the aftermath of my grief. The bond between us has been strengthened. We have not always agreed, but we definitely have been recipients of a miraculous amount of unconditional love for one another. You two girls have a special spot in my heart. God quietly whispered in my ear, "These are your children, and you are their mother." Willow and April will always be a part of our "forever family." I give special recognition to my parents, Johnnie and Joella, my sister, Renee, and my dearly beloved late aunt Flossie. These people were my daily contacts on my journey.

I hope that readers find this book helpful, enjoyable, and informative. If you ever have to endure the loss of a spouse, I hope you find this book encouraging. It is quite okay to cry and laugh during your journey. If you had a strong Christian marriage based upon the love of the Lord and each other, you will enjoy this book.

PROLOGUE

THE VISION

A few days before Ben's death, I had a dream or a vision about one of Ben's deceased family members whom I loved dearly. She and I were traveling the Sun Rail in hopes of attending an awards banquet. Once we arrived, I commented that the recipients were dead, and then I exclaimed to her that she was dead too. She informed me that she was not dead. I looked around and all the "dead people" were jolly and enjoying life while feasting at the banquet. I replied in a perplexed manner that I had a feeling that someone was going to die, and then I inquired as to who it would be. I pleaded with her to tell me who was going to die.

Again, she said, "I'm not dead."

A few days later, but still some days before Ben's death, I told him about the dream and asked for understanding from various family members, including him! It was not until Ben's second day in the hospital that I understood the dream. I awoke to a voice and was reminded about how the disciples were taught to pray "thy kingdom come, thy will be done, on Earth as it is in heaven." Immediately, I understood the dream. It was God's will that Ben would go to heaven, and I had to submit to God's will. I asked God not to allow him to experience pain or suffering, and this was granted! According to the doctors, he slipped away as he slept.

Part 1

The Struggles of Being a Widow

The Challenge of Getting to Know Me

*T*he Julie Andrews song "Getting to Know You" comes to mind. I have not existed as an individual practically all my adult life. I married at eighteen and became a widow at fifty-two. All my adulthood years were spent as a married lady. I have to make a conscious effort to find myself and discover who I really am.

Under the umbrella of depression, finding oneself and one's purpose is like searching for a needle in the haystack. As I grow in God, I am discovering what I am made of. He is equipping me for the road ahead.

Hello

Dear Diary,

My name is Toni Adams, and I am a widow. Within two years, I have had two relapses in the month of December. Just like an alcoholic or an addict, the holidays served as a catalyst in aiding me to spiral out of control. Many times, I've lost track of what I was conversing about. I have locked my keys in the car on countless occasions and forgotten where I parked.

I am overwhelmed by the simplest things and get easily upset. I can burst into tears at the drop of a hat, especially when something is missing, lost, or lacking life. I am a person of beyond-average intelligence. I am well-groomed and pride myself in my overindulgence of perfumes and fragrances. I look normal on the outside, but on the inside, I long for happiness, acceptance, and love. My soul is broken, and I stand at the potter's wheel in pieces that appear to be beyond repair.

Advice

There is nothing too hard for God (Genesis 18:14). Cry, but know within that this is not the end. You have a purpose, and God is not through with you yet. The scriptures tell us, "For I know the thoughts that I think toward you, saith the Lord, thoughts of peace, and not of evil, to give you an expected end" (Jeremiah 29:11).

You Want the Truth or the Lie?

Dear Diary,

When people ask how I am doing, I speak the truth. They want me to reply that I am "fine" and keep moving. Some possess an attitude that seems as if they feel like responding, "Don't take up my time today, sister." They want the lie. The truth is that I am not doing fine. I have ups and downs. I'm sad. I am alone. I have problems concentrating. I am not capable of working. I have lost more than just my husband. I have lost a pastor, a church, and its congregants. The list goes on and on.

Some people want the blow-by-blow details, and others couldn't care less, but there are some who genuinely care. In my depression, I didn't care about their objectives because I felt I was hemorrhaging internally. I needed someone—anyone—to stop the bleeding, bandage me up, and make everything all right. After depression, I came to the startling reality that it is just not good to confide in anyone and everyone.

Advice

Avoid going into detail. However, the basic truth does the soul better than simple lies. I was seeking love, but some people had other motives within their conversations. If you are being questioned as if you been interviewed, it is time to seal your lips. When you speak the truth, speak it in love (Ephesians 4:15).

INVISIBLE

Dear Diary,

Sometimes, I believe I am invisible. People walk by as if they don't see me. They are literally within arm's reach. Perhaps they choose to blind themselves about my brokenness. Maybe they avoid me because they do not have any words of consolation. Perhaps they feel I will want or need something from them, and they aren't in a charitable position or mood. It could very well be that I have nothing to offer them with my newly established, unexpected fixed income.

Could it be my deodorant or my breath? I certainly hope not! Nevertheless, I am in a bubble, trapped in my own world. I place my hand on this wet, enclosed surface, but I cannot feel beyond the enclosure. I scream, but I'm not heard. I am simply invisible.

Advice

Sometimes widows can overwhelm others with their sorrows, and it makes others uncomfortable. Consider your audience. Train yourself to be positive—even in the midst of grief.

The New Me

Dear Diary,

Who am I? I don't know who I am, but I no longer have the status I once had. I am not a wife. I am not a pastor's wife. I am just Toni. Now, I have to get to know exactly who I am. Will I ever return to normalcy? Am I strong enough to weather this storm? Individuality and a new beginning are emerging within me. I hope I can handle this.

Advice

You will begin to establish new traditions without even realizing as the new you transforms.

Who Is My Neighbor?

Dear Diary,

God is using people to help me. Thank You, Lord, for sending some people to help little ole me. It takes a special person to help a widow. I am a person who doesn't have much, and my funds are limited. My neighbors are just phenomenal people. Often, I ask myself, "Who are my neighbors?" My personal definition of a neighbor is similar to Jesus saying, "Woman behold thy son" (John 19:26). The beloved disciple John wasn't her son but would play the role of a son in her life. I never had sons, but God blessed me with brotherly neighbors.

An important note is that all my neighbors aren't in close proximity to me. However, I have had some amazing neighbors who lived near me too. My neighbors have helped me get into my house after locking myself out, mowed my yard, put up a fence, and fixed my air conditioner. They listened to my stories about Ben and comforted my grieving heart. They helped me when I had car trouble and celebrated my victories. Above all, these neighbors happened to be men whose wives allowed them to help me in times of trouble. Their wives were not threatened by me because of my new single/widowed status. I take pride in who I am because I have earned their trust. Luke 10:25–37 sums it up best: a Good Samaritan cares enough to take the time to care.

Advice

Never overlook a man's wife. Express gratitude to her for allowing her husband to help you. A man's wife is your first line of communication.

TO WORK OR NOT TO WORK, THAT IS THE QUESTION

Dear Diary,

People say it is good to work because it keeps you in a routine. I am also told it keeps you busy. However, working is not minimizing my pain, easing my burden, or lessening my heartache. Working is not keeping my mind occupied. Working has become another distraction. In the field of education, specifically teaching, I am responsible for young lives. I must have the ability to think on my feet, grade papers, develop lesson plans, and prepare conferences in advance. I must multitask. I must be a jack of all trades and a master of one. After a careful assessment of my finances, I made a heart-wrenching decision.

Well, thank You for the confirmation, Lord. Girlfriend, a.k.a. Toni Adams, it is time to listen to your conscience and your heart.

Advice

You know when you are not capable of working. Don't wait until someone tells you; instead, tell them. We frequently overlook the warnings of poor mental health. Feeling overwhelmed and full of anxiety are signs that something is wrong. Mental health is important in our day-to-day activities. Even driving a car requires concentration. I have almost had a few accidents due to being preoccupied with my thoughts. Workplaces are starting to realize the need to attend to their employees' mental health situations. Take advantage of psychologists, psychiatrists, twenty-four-hour hotlines employee assistance programs, and short-term disability.

A New Role

*F*alling in love and embracing widowhood is a bit absurd for me. Widows are often lonely, sad, temperamental, and vulnerable. On the other hand, widows can master multitasking, become quite resourceful, and be financially disciplined. A widow's role is always changing. I had never taken the car to the mechanic. I had hardly even paid a bill. I rarely took out the trash. My youngest has officially labeled me a "spoiled brat." I was certainly spoiled, but everything has changed now. Look out, world. Here I come!

WHERE ARE YOU?

Dear Diary,

"Where are you?" are my two daughters' famous words. I just love the role reversal. It makes me laugh sometimes. When they were teenagers, those were *our* famous words. Ben added, "Does your mama know about this?" I think they get it now. Knowing a person's whereabouts is not just about being nosy and controlling; it is a safety issue.

Advice

Share your daily schedule with the people who need to know. This is for your safety. For me, this was my dad, my aunt, my sister, and my daughters who live with me. Finally, keep your cell phone charged. Oh, have some type of roadside assistance in case you are ever stranded.

NIGHTLY RUNS

Dear Diary,

I did not know or realize how much I depended on Ben to make "night runs." I would beg, "Oh, Ben, I really would like a brownie." "Hey, honey, will you please stop and get me an onion on the way from work?" or "It's a good night to go walking on the lakefront together." Now, I don't feel safe going out at night alone. I have no one to run errands for me, spoil me with dessert, or even enjoy the evening with. I must plan to do things before dusk to avoid being raped, robbed, or injured. Maybe it's not that graphic, but you know what I mean.

Advice

Try to run errands during the daylight hours. If you must go out at night, park near lights with the car facing forward to avoid backing out and then moving forward. Have your keys out and avoid distracting activities such as talking on the phone. Above all, remember where you parked. It probably wouldn't hurt to invest in a Taser, gel mace, or a gun for added protection.

SINGLE OR WIDOWED

Dear Diary,

I get it. The light bulb has gone off. For marital status, the categories include married, single, divorced, and widowed. Aren't single, widowed, and divorced still single (alone)? A man informed me that I was single and no longer married. My mouth flung opened, and I snapped, "Me?" I understood that I was alone, but I felt married. Ben had just gone away on a long trip. I still felt emotionally connected to Ben. I have not disconnected from him, and as far as I am concerned, I am still married. However, I realized that I have no physical partner. If you invite me to a party, you no longer see a couple walking through a door. I am single because there is only one of me. My marital status, however, is widowed. In my opinion (as of now), this means I am not available for a relationship because I am still grieving my husband.

Advice

Are we talking numbers or availability? The perception of *single* has a twofold meaning. I found I was always asking for clarity to set the record straight. Slowly, I have started accepting the fact that I can honor my late husband's memory and still long for companionship. It can be a very slow process, likened to a slow leak in a kitchen faucet. Gradually, caring family members gently communicated that moving on is not synonymous with forgetting or dishonoring Ben.

I Am Not the Only Widow

Dear Diary,

I have had the pleasure and displeasure of meeting other widows on an ongoing basis. It's like when you purchase a car and discover that everyone else has it. I am constantly gravitating to widows. The pleasure comes when we have something in common and can identify with each other. The displeasure of meeting widows comes when they are glad their husbands are dead. I failed to understand that some women have suffered domestic violence, drug addiction, alcoholism, and/or infidelity in their marriages prior to becoming widows.

Many times, I feel as though I am in the world but not of the world. No, I am not referring to the Christian connotation. It is more like feeling like an alien. I was a social butterfly before, but I am a loner now. There are days I want to be left alone just to scream it out, cry it out, and pray it out in hopes of feeling better. When I meet another widow, it's a safe place.

My sister introduced me to Grief Share, and I met other people who are just like me. We all thought we were losing our minds at one time or another. I learned that grief brings many emotions (guilt, abandonment, rejection, hopelessness, and so much more). I was taught that grief is just like a fingerprint. There are no two identical ways of grieving. Grief is unique, according to the relationships, time spent, and surrounding circumstances leading to the passing. Even how they passed makes our experiences different.

Advice

Don't be critical about how others grieve. Our job is to support each other through the journey. Fingerprints and snowflakes are all different. No two are the same. Grief is like that too.

IT DIDN'T HAPPEN TO YOU

Dear Diary,

I talked with an acquaintance about some of my troubles. She firmly exclaimed, "If that had happened to me, I would have ..." The fact is that she still has her husband. It did not happen to her, and she really doesn't know how she will react until the time comes. I am intelligent and literally thought I was going crazy some days. Sadly, I am not who I used to be. Despite our differences, there were some pearls of wisdom in our conversation.

Advice

The woman told me to "think practical." I don't know how one does that in these circumstances. I was an emotional wreck. The first year, you just flip. The second year, you are more capable of thinking with sense. Be sure to save money for unexpected catastrophic occurrences such as joblessness due to depression. I noticed that life-changing events spark other life-changing events that you do not necessarily see in the crystal ball. They can be illnesses, financial loss, or changes in family dynamics. We can learn from anyone—even those who are not widows. They may not know anything about being a widow, but they might just know a few things about life and living.

WIDOW TO WIDOW

Dear Diary,

If I could recommend anything of value to widows, I would recommend waiting until change comes. I would warn widows that the Lord is there even though they may not feel Him. Like the story of the footprints in the sand, He is carrying you. I would caution them to save their money as much as possible because they need it to live. In addition, I would advise widows to be careful who they confide in.

I would caution them that their primary loss is their spouse, but secondary losses follow. Both tangible and nontangible losses occur. Tangible losses could be a house, a car, or poor credit. Nontangible losses are emotional support, companionship, relationships, and a spiritual connection with the Lord. I would advise widows to base their decision-making upon godly guidance instead of emotions. Finally, I would say your healing begins with your mind-set and your will to live.

Advice

Just remember, your age, your relationship with your spouse, and the support of family or lack thereof makes every situation unique. Your grief will even be influenced by your relationship with God.

WHAT NOW?

Dear Diary,

Ben was not a fix-it man, but he could get things done. He frequently told me if he couldn't fix something, then he would find someone who could. I had to deal with ant beds in the yard and brakes that don't work on the car. The other day, I needed to mow the lawn and get the house painted to the homeowners' association (HOA) standards. I am still robbing Peter to pay Paul as I juggle this month's bills. I have to get the trash to the curb, put gas in the car, and iron my own clothes. I don't have time to rinse the dew off the car in the morning. That was Ben's job.

Advice

You need a checklist as you assume all your new roles. You will experience role reversal and solo roles simultaneously. Remember to take deep breaths along the way.

It's Mourning Time

I am not sure what is going on in our nation. We live in a world of bizarre behavior, mental illnesses, anger, and sadness. The Grim Reaper seems so real. My heart aches with sadness, my tears carry a burden of grief, and I long for peace, happiness, and love. Ben wasn't killed or gunned down. He didn't die of a drug overdose or take his own life. I have something to be thankful for.

I mourn for Robin Williams (August 11, 2014), Natalie Cole (December 31, 2015), Prince (April 21, 2016), and Bobbi Kristina Brown (July 26, 2015). These celebrities died much too soon. They left us suddenly and without warning, and the suddenness reminded me of Ben. Other people who started their days as usual, but without warning, they fell victim to gun violence. My heart appeared to skip a beat for the nine victims shot in a South Carolina church (June 17, 2015), those in San Bernardino (December 2, 2015), the increasing number of unarmed black men (*Louisiana Weekly*, 2014), and the Pulse shooting (June 12, 2016), which seemed like it occurred in my own backyard.

The officers in blue who vow to protect and defend and were gunned down for no reason saddened my spirit: Wenjian Liu and Rafael Ramos of Brooklyn, New York (2014) and Debra Clayton of Orlando, Florida (2017). There was also the shooting of our government officials in Alexandria, Virginia (2017). Although, Steve Scalise and others survived, I mourned because it was so tragic and senseless. Every time I hear of such tragedies, I mourn for their families and pray for their spouses, children, and relatives. I cannot imagine their pain or their anger.

Ben's grave site.

4:55 A.M.

Dear Diary,

Whether I get two hours of sleep or eight, I always wake up at about five o'clock each morning. It took almost two years before I came to a glaring realization. Ben had his stroke at approximately that time. It is like something wakes me up, and I am expecting another tragedy. Perhaps I have been traumatized by the whole situation. No matter what time I go to sleep, I am up at that time. I feel it necessary to walk around and make sure everyone is all right. Sometimes, I look for signs of breathing among my adult children and grandchildren. Once I witness signs of life, I am content to rest again.

Advice

Prepare yourself for strange occurrence since they are not unusual for widows.

TRIGGERS

Dear Diary,

Certain things trigger me and make me think of Ben. Some memories are fond, and others are dreadful. For instance, I smelled a fragrance Ben wore on another man. I dared not give a compliment for fear it might be crossing a line, but it got my attention. I casually turned my head, and the kind gentleman did not have a clue that I was thinking of a dead man.

The first time I heard sirens after Ben's death was a hurtful reminder of the whole 911 scene that flashed across my mind. I had to compose myself while I was driving. Additionally, when I hear or visit anyone who has had a stroke, I feel compassion for the spouse. The mere mention of the word *stroke* makes me quiver, violently cry, or stop in my tracks. It hurts to even hear the news that someone has suffered a stroke. It all depends on my relationship with the individual or the intensity of my day. On a good note, seeing loving couples reminds me of us.

Advice

Triggers are a part of the process of grief. It is beyond our control—but God. Anniversaries, birthdays, and holidays will trigger emotions. The first time you must "celebrate" alone will trigger a plethora of emotions. Movies and hospital visits can also contribute to spiraling emotions.

Passing by the road Ben traveled on his
way to work evoked many emotions.

DO THE DEAD TALK?

Dear Diary,

I came into this store for something. What was it? I guess I will window-shop until it comes to me. Still nothing! I have lost my train of thought again. I grab a Coke and notice that it reads, "Share a Coke with Ben." That was my husband's name! Thanks for making my day.

Advice

Take delight in knowing that, on some days, you will relish the fact that your loved one is communicating with you. Actually, though, God's Holy Spirit is comforting you.

I DIDN'T FORGET IT'S OUR ANNIVERSARY

Dear Diary,

Today, April 30, 2015, is our anniversary. I cannot sleep. It is 4:00 a.m., and something is telling me to run my fingers across the top of our china cabinet. Ben always kept important things there. I just don't understand why I need to do this in the wee hours of the morning. Needless to say, I will listen to my inner voice. Why is my dog barking uncontrollably while I hear this soft voice? Oh my God! It is an anniversary card from Ben. He had been saving it for our anniversary. The greeting card (Tender Thoughts) expressed that Ben was proud of me, thankful for me, and loved me. It touched my heart. I was mesmerized as streams of water ran down my cheeks. Happy anniversary, Ben! I love you too. I thank you for all that you were to me, and I was so very proud of you. In 1993, the R&B group Tony! Toni! Toné! asked if spouses remember their anniversaries. Apparently, the memo reached heaven—and Ben responded in a big way.

Advice

The Holy Spirit will guide you (John 16:13) and comfort you (John 14:26).

"For making me proud of who you
are and everything you do,
This brings my thanks, my wishes
and special love to you."

Happy Anniversary

(Tender Thoughts)

Surviving versus Living

Dear Diary,

I finally comprehend the meaning of surviving versus living. After Ben's death, I pressed survivor mode. As they say, I "kept it moving." Yes, I went through the motions as if I were a robot. I even fooled myself into thinking I was all right. I tossed and turned each night. I had flashbacks of dialing 911 and him collapsing in my arms and going comatose. Yet everything was all right. I could not go to sleep in our bed because the bedroom now symbolized a tragedy that overshadowed the fond memories and laughter we shared in our room. I hated my home because it was full of memories that made me burst into tears on a consistent basis. Either I ate like a hog or a bird—there was no middle ground. I flashed a smile in the mirror and convinced myself or programmed myself to wear that face at work, while shopping, and even in church. To admit I was sad made me feel defeated. It was surviving—not living. Surviving is a temporary state that allows one to perform satisfactorily. You are able to function even though your mind may not be in the game. You can camouflage your emotions enough to perform the task at hand. From my perspective, survival is a step away from death itself. Survival is a struggle after some type of devastation. Often people say, "Somehow I managed to survive."

After I survived, I sadly died. I could not even shake it off. The telltale signs lurked over me like a scary monster.

I lost my train of thought, spent laborious hours on what could have been accomplished in minutes, and forgot what I was supposed to be doing. That is what grief does! I suffered from a broken heart, an unstable mind, and a fatigued body. I was not suicidal. I had no plan to end my life, but I was not concerned with my health or well-being. I had a "don't-care" attitude. Nothing seemed to cure me during that time. I did not want to live, and I was perfectly okay with God taking me.

During the holiday season, beginning at Thanksgiving, I began to wilt like a flower for two consecutive years. The first year, I grieved over the loss of my husband. The second year, I grieved over the loss of the church he pastored and the severed relationships. The losses were great. The losses seem unexplainable, disappointing, and beyond my control. There is a gaping hole in my heart, but I will get through this in the name of Jesus.

On the other hand, there is living. Jesus came to give us life and to let us live more abundantly (John 10:10). How to live sounds easier than it is done. First, you have to want to live. Some days, I just wanted to stay in my pity party and sit on the mourners' bench. My desire to live was just not there. I was somewhere between life and death.

Finally, I talked myself into living for myself and my loved ones. Living necessitated a plan of action to please God by fulfilling the purpose He had for me. God put joy in my soul. My purpose had not been fulfilled, and I yearned to witness my grandchildren grow into adults. I needed to be a blessing to my parents in their old age. I could be an example to my daughters and nieces of how to conduct themselves as ladies when living alone.

Advice

It is helpful to identify whether you are surviving, dying, or living. God represents life. Subconsciously, I was planning my death. I was physically ill. It was as if I thought my mission on earth had been accomplished. I was acting as if the prophet Isaiah had come into my home and proclaimed that I set my house in order because I was surely going to die (2 Kings 20:1). Little did I know that I would have to help others in similar predicaments heal.

CRAZY OR GRIEVING?

Dear Diary,

In 1971, the Persuaders sang a song about the thin line between love and hate. I think there is a thin line between crazy and grieving, but I happen to know the difference. You are crazy if you have been diagnosed—or maybe even not diagnosed—with a mental disorder that results in rage, violence, major mood swings, or irrational behavior (which may seem demonic at times). You are grieving if you are overcome with sadness that leads to unsound judgement and even minor changes in your behavior. When you compare the two, they look almost identical. Grief is a temporary and short-lived condition. Being crazy tends to be "glued" to a person and lasts a long time. I am not a doctor, but this is my personal experience. If widows aren't careful, we will turn crazy over time. I am sure many will disagree with my analogy, but it is my personal analogy.

Advice

Grief is a season. It too shall pass. However, Christians can go to psychologists and still be Christian. Some people will make you think you only need Jesus. We need Him, but didn't He make those who were a little lower than the angels (Psalm 8:5)? Isn't it possible for the Lord to work through people? Get help!

Truth Is Stranger than Fiction

Dear Diary,

The wind is blowing briskly. That lovely couple Ben married sent a beautiful wind chime as a reminder of his lingering effect on others. On this bright Sunday morning, the chimes are frantically chiming and echoing through our community. Encouraging words about my love have been inscribed on the memorable wind chimes. It speaks of God welcoming him to his new home. It tells us the bells symbolize a twofold meaning. The chimes ring in celebration and serve as a reminder that we will be united again.

Maybe Ben is saying, "You are late, Toni!" Even though he is not here, he still wants me to be on time for morning service. Wow! He still speaks.

Advice

Take heed and listen to the little things.

BATTLE SCARS

Dear Diary,

If you fought in a war, you may have been attacked. If so, you are blessed to have survived. I see grief as a battle. It's a battle of the mind, heart, and spirit. It is spiritual warfare going on from within. It's in my mind. I revisit that dreadful day when I called 911. I revisit the week prior to Ben's death like a replayed movie. I remember him sharing his vision of the church with me in the days before his death. I reflect on how hard he worked to please his family. I smile when I recall him making my yard beautiful days before his passing. I delight that we celebrated our youngest daughter's first year in the navy, the twins' first birthday party, Father's Day, and the Fourth of July in the weeks before Ben passed away. It's a matter of the heart. I have a broken heart, a heavy heart, a lost love, and a lifetime of memories. It makes my heart ache, and I long to recover. My soul is in conflict with the emotions of bereavement.

Survivors of war still bear the scars and wounds. Injuries go through a healing process. They do not disappear with the snap of a finger. Wounds first need cleansing. Pressure to stop the bleeding may be required. If there is depth to a wound, there may be a need for surgery or even amputation. Of course, there is recovery time. Aftercare is crucial to prevent infection from setting in. Infection can worsen a condition or reverse the healing cycle.

Advice

Well-wishers may have great advice for you, but you may not be at that stage of your healing. Aspire to get there—but don't deny where you are. The scars remain. Even Jesus, once He arose, had scars in His hands, feet, and side. Scars are a reminder of what you've overcome (John 20:26–28). They allow us to delight in what God has done and give us stronger testimonies.

Scars can result from any war. However, when the battle is over, I will be healed, restored, and resurrected. The women's conference at this church proclaimed victory for "princess warriors."

Rejected Stone

O ne of the strongest forces other than depression (for me) was the spirit of rejection. After all this crying, grieving, and loss, I was going to be rejected too? Yes! Expect to have enemies disguised as friends. People are quite amazing before, during, and after funerals and weddings. As a matter of fact, the two celebratory events are often mistakenly referred to interchangeably. Why? Well, in a marriage, when two become one, it means that someone lost their hierarchy of power and inclusiveness. The funeral is symbolic of the exact same thing. In addition to the person who is gone, other factors have vanished. There has been a transfer of power in decision-making, influence, and finance. Just like in a marriage, there may be name changes on bank accounts and business matters. Instead of playing jointly, you are now a soloist. Your name is no longer connected by the conjunctions *and* or *or*. Marriage is for better or worse and until death you part. Death brings out the better and worse of people until disagreements do part us. Some will not like the proverbial new sheriff in town and the power you hold. However, because they are aware of the power you possess, they can pretend quite well. The best comparison I have is an adulterous man or woman who strikes up an argument just to go and commit adultery. After death, some people want to part ways with you—and now they have a reason.

Rejection does not necessarily mean you did anything wrong. On the contrary, people who are rejected are often people who make godly decisions, abide by the law, are leaders, and work for the betterment of others. What did Jesus do to anyone? He healed the sick, raised the dead, drove demons out of a lunatic, and did so much more. Yet, in one week, they hailed Him in high esteem and graced His presence with palms (Matthew 21: 6–11). Just a week later, they shouted, "Crucify Him" (Mark 15:13). The torture continued with denial and betrayal from His chosen disciples. That's not even all of it. He was whipped, crowned with thorns, and nailed to a cross. When He thirsted for water, He was given vinegar (John 19:28–30). If I am Christlike, why did I expect to escape it? Well, I didn't escape. Jesus was despised and rejected. He was a man of sorrows and was acquainted with grief (Isaiah 53:3). When you have a clear conscience because you did what was right to please the Lord, you will be given peace. Rejected stones become the head of the corner (Matthew 21:42).

Now What?

Dear Diary,

After the funeral, what happens when the crowd is gone? Well, the phone calls will cease, friends will vanish, and some will fall out with you. I'm just sayin'!

Advice

Ask yourself a few questions: Who calls and checks on you? What are their goals? What will they gain? What will you gain? The best gains I have experienced have been hope and encouragement. However brief the communication, if it lifted my spirit, put a smile on my face, or caused my heart to sing, I gained.

You Couldn't Wait?

Dear Diary,

Jesus seemed so disgusted with Peter and the two sons of Zebedee because they couldn't wait one hour as he prayed in the Garden of Gethsemane. It had not even been three years, but they couldn't wait until I was healed. It makes me feel a bit crunchy, but I probably should not because Jesus's handpicked disciples couldn't wait one hour (Matthew 26:40). The Bible states that Jesus was already sorrowful and heavy (Matthew 26:37), yet He lacked the requested support.

Advice

Don't hold it against the people—turn it over to God. Jesus prayed in the Garden of Gethsemane just before He was crucified, but didn't He rise? We have resurrection power in His name. Watch and pray that you will enter not in temptation for the spirit is willing but the flesh is weak (Matthew 26:41).

NEGATIVE PEOPLE GOT TO GO!

Dear Diary,

Pardon my language, but negative people got to go. Whether family, friend, or foe, if you are negative, you got to go! I cannot not heal among this type of person. My problems are much too big to be a part of anything that subtracts, empties from my aching heart, or interferes with my walk with the Lord. My pastor preaches that everything that occurs in life is for our good, our growth, and His glory. I had blinders on in the beginning, but now I have my eyes open to the truth of the matter. It's all about my healing.

Advice

Widows can be negative too, which is all the more reason to come out from among them. Prior to my husband's passing, I was a lemonade maker. I saw the glass as half-full. I was a positive person. Suddenly, I experienced a domino effect.

All hope is not lost because your loved one has passed. Your negative attitude toward life must go too. It's all about your healing. With that said, my home speaks to positivity. I wake up in the morning to decorative pillows with positive messages: "My happy place," Love you more," and "Glam-ma." My flameless candles say "Love, laugh, and live." On my fireplace, I have the letters P-E-A-C-E. In my kitchen, a sign reads: "Share a Coke and a smile." The dinette area displays a lighthouse. Messages in my bedroom read "Believe, Pray, Ask, and Receive," "Education is the key," and "Teachers make all other professions possible."

My home speaks positivity.

VICTIMIZED

If you think people will feel sorry for you, think again. You may be the victim. Mechanics may create problems for your car since they know there is no man in your home. Some people feel they can bully, scold, embarrass, or be demeaning toward you because they know that no man will confront them. You are unprotected by a husband. Even your children may become unruly because there is no masculine leadership in the home. In other words, they may try you. Since Daddy is gone, they think you will become a pushover. People, in general, know they only have to deal with you since Papa Bear will not come knocking on their door. I wonder what Ben thinks while looking down from above.

As for me, I have made up mind. From this day forth, I will write letters of complaint, gently hang up the phone, walk away, and call law enforcement (if I must), but I will no longer be your victim. On the contrary, I must maintain Ben's legacy of strength because he has passed the baton to me.

Advice

The Bible warns that people should avoid taking advantage of widows (Exodus 22:22–24). As widows, it is important to remember that God is our father, protector, and deliverer. Let Him fight your battles and know that the battle is not yours but His (2 Chronicles 20:15).

THE ISLAND OF MISFIT TOYS

On the Island of Misfit Toys, there's a bird that does not fly, a cowboy who rides an ostrich, a boat that does not stay afloat, a spotted elephant, a bird that swims, and a Charlie-in-the-box. My all-time favorite was Rudolph, the reindeer with the shining nose that saved Christmas. However, Dolly for Sue was less popular. Some disagreement has arisen as to why Dolly, the cute red-haired doll with the pleasing personality did not quite fit in on the island. A misfit can appear to be normal. Dolly for Sue might have had an inner problem. Some believe she suffered from depression. Therefore, her problem was not visible.

Generally, misfits are noticeably different, unfulfilling of their purpose, or ill constructed, such as the train with square wheels. In *Rudolph the Red-Nosed Reindeer*, the islanders have been unwanted for quite a while. The misfits will remain on the island until someone wants them.

I stayed on an island, and God sent people to me who have only known me as a misfit—but they still wanted me. Those people had just met me, but they accepted me in my struggle to regain normalcy.

Advice

God exclaimed that the wheat and the tare will grow together and He will do the separating (Matthew 13:30). It's not just on Judgment Day! When we are enduring hardship and trials, He chooses to separate us from certain people, places, and things. Instead, He joins us with other people, places, and things. It is amazing! What the devil meant for my bad, God turned it around for our good (Genesis 50:20).

IN-LAWS, EX-LAWS, AND OUTLAWS

Dear Diary,

I have noticed that a widow's relationship within her deceased husband's family can be categorized as either an in-law, an ex-law, or an outlaw. The categorization is on an individual basis and may or may not reflect the views of the family at large. I guess every family—publicly or secretly—does this before death. Those who are in-laws still view you as part of their family and treat you as such. In other words, the death of a spouse has no bearing on the relationship between the two parties. Ex-laws are like exes. You are no longer a part of the family. We all know that exes can be cordial or horrible. Nevertheless, you used to be related to them—and that is that! Outlaws are the worse. They are done with you. It is almost like you never existed. They exclude you from family events, often avoid speaking to you, and appear tense in your very presence. The length of the marriage or the number of children you have does not matter when someone feels you no longer belong.

Advice

Rather than acting in an ungodly way, remove yourself from volatile situations. Martin Luther King Jr. reminded us that, the law cannot make anyone love us. Only God can change the hearts of humankind. The law can only make them respect you. Celebrate those you have left. Those who love you unconditionally exhibit God's love, and that's a true blessing.

Celebrating the joys of the season
with one of my special in-laws.

THESE THREE

Dear Diary,

It really hurts my heart to express my recent observances, especially since I'm a former pastor's wife. The book of Corinthians speaks volumes as it relates to how Christians ought to behave. Paul instructed the church of Corinth to love one another. One of my favorite scriptures within 1 Corinthians is the thirteenth chapter. As a former first lady or pastor's wife of a church, I have encountered all kinds of people from many walks of life. I love people and consider myself a people person.

I have also noticed that we are more title driven, at times, than Christian driven. Title-driven people are often power hungry and partakers of a "have-and-have-not" attitude within the church. Titles define our duties within a church, but they do not define us. Titles do not grant us a fast track to the kingdom. Heaven is not some theme park where you skip over the little people (like me) because of "somebodiness." Sometimes, our titles and our behaviors just don't line up. There is a striking difference between being religious and being Christian. Being religious is ritualistic and carries a great concern with position or status in the church rather than the inner soul. Christianity is inward behavior that radiates.

We live in a world of competiveness, ulterior motives, jealously, and deceit. Yes! It is in the church. After all, wasn't Paul writing about a church with its own set of unique problems? I am reminded of Ricky Ricardo's reply to Lucy after she had been caught in her devilment: "Lucy, you've got some 'splaining to do." Church, we have some explaining to do. Where is the love? Paul instructed us, after his vivid examples of love that three things remain. "And now abideth faith, hope, charity, these three; but the greatest of these is charity" (1 Corinthians 13:13).

Advice

Love is not puffed up nor does it behave unseemingly (1 Corinthians 13:4–5). Love is not easily provoked (1 Corinthians 13:5). Love is not envious (1 Corinthians 13:4). Many churchgoers have the love of Christ. I have been blessed to see this love in action. I've also seen people who allow a title to take precedence over pleasing God. Back in the day, we called it having a swollen head. They are too busy doing them and don't have time for you. Their priority is themselves. When you reach out to them, don't be surprised. Ask God to allow you to be humble and not driven by a title.

Sometimes, even widows get stuck in their titles. A widow is often viewed as a pitiful, sad, hopeless person. If we are not careful, we will stay there and never heal from those connotations. It can easily happen to any of us. God is not concerned with our titles, degrees, or accolades. He does not love you any less for being a widow than He would an esteemed church official. Let's think about the people He went to heal and comfort. Faith, hope, and love are necessary for the journey ahead. Remember what love is according to the scriptures and know that love never fails (1 Corinthians 13:8). "Keep thy heart with all diligence for out of it are the issues of life" (Proverbs 4:23).

Part 2

THE BUSINESS SIDE
OF BEING A WIDOW

Dotting Every I and Crossing Every T

*I*t is such a massive shift, and at times, it can feel like a bit much. Financial restrictions are done by choice, habit, or circumstance. They can be planned or unplanned. These have become necessary statements for me:

- I choose to "live" differently.
- I am on a fixed income.
- Some things do not fit into my budget.
- I am in the process of downsizing.
- What are the basics?
- Could you put that in writing with a signature and date?
- I am presently not in a position to loan money.
- I will have to consult my lawyer before even considering this (even though I may not have one).

- This is not beneficial and requires me to live above my means.
- Do I have disability insurance on this?
- My charity of choice is my church, and it requires tithing and offering.
- This is not working today.
- While I support others, I do not commit myself to allocate funds elsewhere.

This is what I call "smart talk." If these or similar phrases are not a part of your vocabulary, they will quickly become a source of life and help you protect your assets, maintain shelter, and bear the necessities of life. Ben told me the next power scripture for the church was Psalm 118:17: "I shall not die, but live, and declare the works of the Lord."

I died in so many ways due to being stuck in my feelings. Now, I count my blessings and make wise choices. I invest in me, my children, and grandchildren (to a point). I invest in those who give me life. I think before I make commitments.

A Widow's Might

Dear Diary,

I purposely sought the scriptures that relate to widows. I really don't think I gave them much thought until I became a widow. James 1:27 reminds the church of its responsibility to widows and orphans. The widow of Zarephath (1 Kings 17:13–15) obeyed Elijah and ate during the famine.

Ben and I were always givers, and I continued to give to others after his death. If I saw a need, I gave. To an extent, I might have done this because Ben would have approved. I failed to realize I would be living on less, and I didn't foresee that my depression would affect my ability to work. Once I started depleting my resources, I asked God to not let that quench my giving. I continue to tithe and give offering to the church. Then, out of nowhere, God told me to give more. The Lord gently whispered to me that I needed to give to my pastor and his wife each month for an entire year. *With what? How? You sure this is You, God?* Even though these two people really didn't know me—and vice versa—God wanted me to pour into them. When I think about it, God used them to fill the hole I had within. He wanted me to respect their spiritual leadership and recognize the enormous role they played in my healing. What did they do that was so special for me? They preached the Word of God. They spoke words of encouragement. They seemed to care for one of the least ones (that would be me). God gives us pastors according to His heart (Jeremiah 3:15).

Jesus observed those giving in the treasury (Mark 12:40–44). The rich gave a little in comparison to their wealth, but the poor widow gave all she had. I was in a state of a financial loss. Without working I have paid $500 or more per month for health coverage. After health coverage rose for the third time, I had to let it go. I prayed that my good health would last. God has provided for my needs. I am grateful! Glory be to God for the things He has done!

I obeyed the Lord, and I never lacked anything. The very next year, I landed a full-time job with health benefits! My health was restored, and my depression was history. My heart is filled with praise!

Advice

I never regret anything I gave, because I gave from my heart or out of obedience. I gave when I needed it most and sacrificed, but God had to show me how He was in control. All I can say—"Won't He do it?" "Every man according as he purposeth in his heart, so let him give; not grudgingly, or of necessity: for God loveth a cheerful giver" (2 Corinthians 9:7).

Checklist

Dear Diary,

Death can be so sudden. We are here today and gone tomorrow. It is no wonder that the Bible compares our lives to grass. In the morning, it flourishes, and in the evening, it is cut down (Psalm 90:5–6). The Bible compares life to vapor (James 4:14). We are here for a short time, and then we vanish.

In preparation for death, you may need to get a few things in order:

- a will
- a burial space
- a beneficiary
- a beneficiary for bank accounts
- a health care surrogate
- a power of attorney
- a living will
- a safe-deposit box for important documents
- mortgage insurance
- trusts

Advice

This is the beginning of a checklist that can be beneficial to those who are left behind. An attorney is a good friend during widowhood. A will does not prevent one from going to probate.

Smart Investments

Dear Diary,

It was brought to my attention that I have been working in the field of education for a whopping twenty-nine years, and I am not yet sixty. This is quite a milestone, and I give thanks to God. I attended a few sessions to get me educated, and I learned a few things. I will be able to receive one Social Security check at the designated time. Of course, the higher of the two will be my choice. I can open a trust or college fund for the grandchildren. I can decide to invest in tax-deferred accounts that cannot be touched by creditors and will not be included in probate. I even learned that you can list the items or family heirlooms within your home that you want given to specific people and get it notarized. In my particular situation, having beneficiaries under twenty-five creates limitations on my retirement pension when I die. I am still planning on working another five years, but I have to consider, ponder, and pray over many things.

Advice

Attend seminars to become educated concerning your situation, including estate planning, investing, and preparation for retirement. After becoming a widow, it is vitally necessary to document your requests. Without specific documentation, your family can fight over your assets and acquire excessive attorney fees.

Documentation solidifies your decisions, but involving a lawyer will ensure that your desires are fulfilled. Your family may appear to agree with your decisions in your presence, but they may think differently after your death.

SHOW ME THE MONEY

Dear Diary,

In retrospect, I understand that making money decisions while under emotional distress does not always make sense. As a widow, I was afraid that I would go without or would gradually lose things. Sometimes, you just feel like you're in the business of loss. The words *foreclosure* and *repossession* literally make me shake.

I failed to realize that the true source of money is God. He that trusteth in his riches shall fall (Proverbs 11:28). Without the Lord, neither my husband nor I would have been able to obtain our possessions. I knew those things all along, but now that I'm husbandless, I have a new perspective. I stopped doing the math for my operating budget. I come up short every time, but God provides the overflow.

It took a minute to pull myself together and comprehend the full power of God. Ben is no longer my leaning post or financial adviser. I have to go right to the power source. I must go to Jesus for myself. I pray over my money and ask God to make me a good steward over any and all funds He provides me. I ask Him to control my impulsive spending and show me how to save money for a rainy day. I also ask Him to multiply it. If my dear aunt Sister can ask the Lord to multiply our food at a family meal (when we were not prepared for the extra guests), I surely can ask Him to multiply it. If the Lord can feed five thousand men with two fish and five barley loaves (Luke 9: 14–17), I can send a shout-out for Jesus to multiply it. Boy, the blessings within those fragments have left me spellbound.

Advice

Until you have reached your spiritual growth spurt and emotional stability, realize that your money decisions may go awry. Pray over your money. Ask for godly guidance and self-control in your spending. Do not become imprisoned or enslaved to money and what you view as limitations. God will show you what He can do with money.

Record It or Write It Down

Dear Diary,

I had no idea how money, greed, and power could play such powerful roles in death, but they do. This entire process can be hurtful and lead to destructive relationships. It speaks of dishonesty, wrecked characters, and mistrust. It is the catalyst of jealousy and malice. It is no wonder the Bible states the lover of money is the root of all evil (1 Timothy 6:10). The O'Jays knew what they were singing about for sure. I have not experienced this ugliness directly, but I have heard the stories and lived vicariously through the experiences of other widows.

Advice

When there is a sense of urgency, record important legal decisions. You may want to video everyone in the room and say, "All in favor say aye, and those opposed say nay." It sounds like a church business meeting, but it may be a saving grace in the long run. Let technology work for you. Save text messages, voice messages, and other important conversations that solidify your decision-making process. When signing documents, recruit nonrelatives if possible. Protect your spouse's wishes in a legal manner as best you can.

A WIDOW'S VOCABULARY WORDS

Dear Diary,

Here are a few words to know as it relates to a widow's business concerns:

- alone
- beneficiary
- claim
- death certificate / disinherited spouse
- elective share / estate
- financial adviser
- godly guidance
- health care surrogate
- insurance / identity theft
- joint account
- keepsakes
- lawyer / living will
- mental state of loved one / money market
- next of kin
- obituary
- payable on death / permission / probate
- quitclaim deed
- retirement benefits
- Social Security benefits
- trust (financially speaking and morally speaking)/taxes
- under the advice of a professional
- videotape/vulnerable

- warfare/will
- x (examine motives)
- your legal rights
- *zzzzzzz* (get rest)

Advice

Get to know your rights as a spouse. If your assets are together, it will be ideal. I thank God every day that this was the least of my worries. However, not all married couples share their assets. Whether a couple is at odds or separated at the time of death, a spouse is entitled to a certain percentage of the assets. This makes it extremely important to know the laws that apply to your state.

Part 3

THE MIRACULOUS POWER OF GOD'S HEALING

Metamorphosis

*A*s I grasped this unfamiliar place, I came to the startling conclusion that my life had taken a sudden and drastic transformation. I suddenly became the breadwinner, the decision maker, and the CEO of the household. If I wanted anything, I literally had to go out and get it. My choices would either add to or take away from the household expenditures and its operation. I am also the spiritual leader and my own personal cheerleader. A butterfly experiences a metamorphosis in its third stage. Prior to metamorphosis, it lives in a dark cocoon or chrysalis where it is nourished for some time. When it emerges, it is wrapped in brilliant color, full of life, and eventually begins to spread its wings and fly. It's time to fly! "I shall not die, but live, and declare the works of the Lord" (Psalm 118:17). I lived in darkness and have been nourished in the Word of God. Now, it is time for my metamorphosis.

I am a butterfly spreading my wings.

The CEO of this household has decided to get her house painted and spruced up.

THE ABCS OF WIDOWHOOD

Dear Diary,

The Jackson 5's "ABC" has nothing on this!

- As for me and my house, we will serve the Lord (Joshua 24:15).
- Beauty for ashes (Isaiah 61:3).
- Casting all you care upon Him; because He careth for you (1 Peter 5:7).
- Delight thyself also in the Lord and He shall give you the desires of thy heart (Psalm 37:4).
- Every knee shall bow to me and every tongue confess to God (Romans 14:11).
- For God so loved the world, that He gave His only begotten Son that whosoever believeth in Him should not perish, but have everlasting life (John 3:16).
- God has not given us the spirit of fear; but of power, and of love, and of a sound mind (2 Timothy 1:7).
- How excellent is thy loving kindness, O God! Therefore the children of men put their trust under the shadow of thy wing (Psalm 36:7).
- I can do all things through Christ which strengtheneth me (Philippians 4:13).
- Jesus wept (John 11:35).
- Knock and it shall be opened unto you (Matthew 7:7).

- Love your enemies, bless them that curse you, do good to them that hate you, and pray for them which despitefully use you and persecute you (Matthew 5:44).
- Make a joyful noise unto the Lord, all ye lands (Psalm 100:1).
- No weapon that formed against me shall prosper (Isaiah 54:17).
- O taste and see that the Lord is good: blessed is the man that trusteth in Him (Psalm 34:8).
- Pray without ceasing (1 Thessalonians 5:17).
- Watch ye, stand fast in the faith, quit you like men, be strong (1 Corinthians 16:13).
- Rejoice in the Lord alway: and again I say, rejoice (Philippians 4:4).
- Serve the Lord with gladness: come before His presence with singing (Psalm 100:2).
- The Lord is my shepherd; I shall not want (Psalm 23:1).
- And the peace of God, which passeth all understanding, shall keep your hearts and minds through Christ Jesus (Philippians 4:7).
- Verily, verily, I say unto thee, Except a man be born of the water and of the Spirit, he cannot enter into the kingdom of God (John 3:5).
- Weeping endureth for a night, but joy cometh in the morning (Psalm 30:5).
- Examine yourselves, whether ye be in the faith; prove your own selves. Know ye not your own

selves, how that Jesus Christ is in you, except ye be reprobates? (2 Corinthians 13:5).
- Ye are the light of the world. A city that is set on a hill cannot be hid (Matthew 5:14).
- Zarephath the widow (1 Kings 17).

Advice

Latch on to a scripture and remember it verbatim. In hard times, repeat it until you believe and receive it. When Ben was my pastor, he referred to this as a "power scripture." I am a witness that this is powerful and mind changing.

PRUNING

Dear Diary,

Have you ever thought about a tree that appears dead, dormant, and dry during the winter? Its severely dry branches make it look dead. We, as humans, can look like that from the inside. Spiritual deadness is a for-real place. When you lose communication with God, your prayer life ceases or decreases. Your values may not satisfy God. You can avoid or forsake yourself from assembling with God's people. People need pruning too. The dead branches need to be trimmed, cut, or sawed down to allow for growth. God, in His infinite wisdom, does the pruning. It took me quite a while to understand why I did not feel God. He had not distanced Himself from me. By wallowing in depression, I drifted away. I still attended church, but I was lacking the leadership of a pastor for an entire year. Thankfully, I was spiritually in tune enough to grab hold of myself.

I began to seek Him in the midst of my storm. "I once was blind, but now I see" ("Amazing Grace"). "I came to Jesus as I was weary, worn, and sad. I found in Him a resting place, and He has made me glad" ("I Heard the Voice of Jesus Say"). Some people compare it to removing the layers of an onion. The most important takeaway I understand about pruning is that it is seasonal. Pruning prepares one for growth, renewal, and life.

Advice

Stay connected to Jesus. Surround yourself with spiritual-minded people. Saturate yourself with godly messages, lessons, and inspirational readings. Display messages of hope and healing in your home.

This tree needs pruning.

Since the dead branches have been eliminated, this tree will grow.

There Are Two Kinds of People in the World

Dear Diary,

Back in the day, I used to watch *The Flip Wilson Show* (1970–1974). Geraldine was a sassy fashionista who would often say, "The devil made me do it." The show depicted a genuine portrayal of what being human is all about. Each of us have two sides, and one is generally more dominant than the other. However, no matter how good we are, we can cross over to the other side.

There are two kinds of people in the world. In my state of depression, I crossed the fence for sure. I also witnessed others doing likewise. Right is always right, and wrong is always wrong. Regardless of who we are, we are much better when we no longer advocate for anyone (including ourselves) in our wrongness. Dr. Martin Luther King Jr. said, "The time is always right to do what is right." Drum roll, please. I present the two kinds of people:

- givers and takers
- problem makers and problem solvers
- positive and negative
- visionaries and the dreamless
- the haves and the have-nots

- troublemakers and peacemakers
- those who start and those who finish

Advice

When you are on the wrong side, straighten up in the name of Jesus.

Is It the Devil or God?

Dear Diary,

Everything bad that happens is not because of the devil. I think about Job (Job 1:8). Who tested his faith? What about Shadrach, Meshach, and Abednego? If Nebuchadnezzar hadn't thrown them in the fiery furnace, we would never have known and understood that God will stand with us—even in a blazing fire (Daniel 3:24–25). Our trials, infirmities, and lots in life reveal what we are made of. They unveil what side of the fence we are on. It reminds me Alan Wong's *Are You a Carrot, an Egg, or a Coffee Bean?* The carrot enters boiling water hard and exits soft. The egg enters boiling water with some fluidity but solidifies. The coffee bean goes into boiling water alone and self-contained. It dispels and changes the entire atmosphere around it. As a matter of fact, it leaves a noticeable and lingering aroma. Over and over, God shows us that He will give us favor in His time and His season if we do what's right by Him.

Advice

Jacob wrestled with an angel to gain his blessing. Don't let go until God blesses you. You may have a limp after the battle, but you still can walk in your blessing (Genesis 32:25).

THANK YOU, LORD

Dear Diary,

Thank You, Jesus! In spite of it all, I still thank You. I know things could be worse. I am still living and moving. Through hurt, disappointment, and grieving, I get it. You have my front, back, and in between. I cannot thank You enough. After so many could haves, would haves, and should haves, I am still standing. I may be a bit wobbly at times, but I am still here.

Advice

Begin the day by thanking God.

SHALL WE DANCE?

My granddaughter and I often dance together. Wow! I can't tell whose smile is the widest. Is it mine or hers? She enjoys Grandma, and I enjoy her. Her twin brother is my practical joker. He is always stealing Grandma's seat or doing something to make me chase him around the house. My youngest granddaughter likes me to rock her to sleep and cuddle. My grandchildren who live in California are my FaceTime buddies, and we enjoy making silly faces, animating our voices, and the sheer company of each other. I want to leave them more than a memory or an inheritance. I need to leave them the legacy of how to behave as Christians despite their problems, perceptions from others, and diverted plans.

Advice

It's okay to be silly and laugh. Love each grandchild for who they are. Children are a gift from God (Psalm 127:3–5).

Meet Grandma's dancer (left) and
rocking chair partner (right).

My daughter, Willow, with Grandma's practical joker.

My daughter, April, with Grandma's California baby.

My FaceTime grandson.

How Much Do I Owe?

Dear Diary,

Owing is a form of repayment that is often associated with money. The Lord allowed me to borrow my husband. He belonged to God even before he was assigned to his parents. Because God loaned me my husband, I owe God something. Christians owe God their appreciation for loaning us our loved ones. Through tears, restless nights, and utterly confusion, I may get distracted. However, I must not forget the Giver, our Lord and Savior, Jesus Christ. The Lord gave His life for me, and I owe Him my life. As shattered as my heart is and as clouded as my mind may be, God still wants me. He is my Savior! As I strive to live, I owe Him my time, energy, money, and life.

Advice

"Amazing Grace" is not just a hymn. It is a soul-stirring Christian reality. He saved a wretch like me.

MEMORY LANE

Dear Diary,

It is always fun when my daughters say, "Remember when Daddy ..." or "What did Daddy used to say?" I wouldn't trade it for anything.

Advice

Share the fun times and laugh. There are many ways to preserve memories. Some use articles of clothing from their spouses to create memory quilts, pillows, or teddy bears.

Ben and I (far left) are at a Justice for Trayvon Rally.
Source: *Sanford Herald*
March 25, 2012
Photos by Rome Guzman

April's graduation
May 2013

Willow's wedding day.

Church installs Rev. Adams

Participating in the installation service are (from left) Rev. and Mrs. Benjamin Adams Jr., Rev. A. ... Brown, James Linn, Mayor ... and Undersheriff Steve ...

Jazz fest today

Hat elegance today

Fondly remembering our official
day as pastor and first lady.
Sanford Herald—March 28, 1993

Church honors Rev. Adams

By Marva Hawkins
Herald Correspondent

The Rejected Stone Full Mission non-denominational Christian church family honored their pastor and first lady, Sunday, June 24, in the Sanford Civic Center.

The Rev. Benjamin and Toni Adams Jr., were surprised with an appreciation dinner. Members, family and friends were on hand to pay tribute to the honorees.

Elder Calvin C. Donaldson was mistress of ceremonies for the occasion.

The entrance of the honorees was greeted with a chorus of "surprise, surprise" from the guests. Oh, what a look of surprise was shown on their faces.

Musical selections were rendered by the Spirit of Life Singers and Pastor Charles Graham of Orlando. Invocation was given by Minister Tommy Gatlin, with scripture by Minister Cecil Cannady and words of welcome by Edmond Washington. Sharron Cannady gave the occasion. Greetings were given on behalf of Mayor Brady Lessard, and Deputy Sheriff Steve Harriett of the Seminole County Sheriff's department.

Expressions of love and appreciation were expressed by the Rev. William Lewis, Elder Calvin Donaldson, Deacon Oscar Redden and Deacon Calvin Mosley.

After a delicious dinner, the honorees were recognized with a tribute from Katoya Raynor in a Praise Dance routine. Little Lhaylor Jordan, Rejected Stone's youngest member, recited the 23rd Psalm.

Plaques, proclamations from City Commissioner Velma Williams, Turner Clayton, NAACP, Brothers Keepers and Oscar Redden, were all presented to Pastor Adams for his outstanding community service.

Presentations on behalf of the church where Pastor Adams has pastored for eight years were presented by Chairperson Rosella Fields and the Rejected Stone Church family. The honorees were given a suit and accessories for Benjamin and first lady Adams.

They were blessed with a mini Florida vacation.

The Rev. Benjamin and Toni Adams Jr.

Dinner table not place for battle of wills

Today I remember Ben with admiration.
Source: *Sanford Herald - July 8, 2001*

Saying Farewell

I have often heard that it's not over until God says it's over. Well, God has definitely showed me that it's over. Ben and I are no longer a couple. I can no longer hold his hands or wrap my arms around him. I know these things, but I can't say goodbye. I feel his heartbeat and his presence. How do I say goodbye to thirty-four years of my life? How do I go on pretending it never existed? I see his clothes and smell his fragrance, but he is not here. It is difficult to depart from possessions and bury other things.

MY WEDDING RINGS

Dear Diary,

I am a married woman, and I proudly wear my rings on my finger. I am not available, and I am very much in love with Ben. I still talk to him daily. I will wear these rings until my dying days—at least that is what I thought. I pictured myself wearing those rings forever.

I am not sure why my engagement ring started to lose diamonds every week. I have officially lost five diamonds now, and my ring looks like a snaggletooth six-year-old. I was in a tizzy and went to three jewelers. The first jeweler told me he couldn't fix it because of its invisible setting. The second jeweler said he could fix it for $250. My goodness— are they replacing diamonds with cubic zirconia? The third jeweler could repair the ring for four grand. This seems like Goldilocks and the Three Bears. Which one is just right? I don't want cubic zirconia. I cannot afford four grand, and the other jeweler can't fix it. I don't know what to do, but wearing a ring with all those missing diamonds ain't working.

Advice

Some widows wear their wedding rings for the memories. Some wear their rings to remain connected (like I did). Others remove them to have closure and come to grips with their widowed status. Then, there are people like me whose diamonds fall out of their rings—and they have to make a decision.

My snaggle-toothed engagement ring.

HIS STUFF

Dear Diary,

Ben's stuff stays until I make up my mind that it goes. I do not want anyone to help me get rid of his stuff. I'll do this when I'm good and ready. Well, the time has come. I got everything out of the closets and drawers and put it into bins until I can decide what to do. I gather all Ben's shoes and put them in a pile. I am exhausted physically and emotionally. I can no longer move. Okay, I will go to sleep and then go to work the next morning. Night-night, Ben.

I wake up the next morning, see the pile of shoes, and stumble over them. It is a painful reminder that he is gone. I am sobbing and in no shape to work. I cry all the way there, wiping my tears away, and flash a smile as if everything is all right.

Advice

There are many things you can do with his stuff. You can pay it forward. I gave the men in the family a piece of Ben's personal belongings for the first Christmas. You can donate or pawn items. Tools that you never will use can be pawned. Of course, you will want to keep keepsakes and photos. Some things may need to be trashed. I trashed a missing cuff link or sock and chuckled. *I wonder what Ben did with the other one?*

GOOD NIGHT

Dear Diary,

Ben was a romantic. He spent countless time and energy selecting clothing he wanted me to have. Whether it was a vacation getaway, Valentine's Day, or just a special occasion, he shopped for what he wanted. It was so cute when he asked my approval. After his passing, I stumbled across a drawer of apparel. I examined them one by one. Nobody talks about what to do with personal articles of clothing. Where is the book for that one? Those little articles of clothing were so sentimental. It would be a shame to trash them. Still, it is not like I can give them away to anyone. Bingo! I got an idea. Gone!

Advice

Whatever you decide to do with your personal wear, say good night to it and get rid of it.

THE BEDROOM

Dear Diary,

The room, our room, is a crime scene to me. Anytime I visit there, I have a flashback of holding Ben's lifeless body in the bow of my arm. I frantically called 911 and prayed for God to raise Ben like He raised Lazarus. I could hear myself talking. I was weeping as I answered all the questions on the dispatcher's list. I witnessed Ben taking what seemed like his final breath and then witnessed him drifting into a deep sleep. As a matter of fact, he was snoring. I could never have imagined what I would endure all by myself. Ben was snoring in my arms, unaware of any existence in the world. I fought back the tears. I knew he was gone, but I refused to believe he was leaving me. *This is not happening to me!*

This is the "the room" where it all took place. Two years later, I still can't sleep in that room or even stay there too long. There are too many memories.

Advice

If you cannot sleep in your room, don't worry. In God's time, He will lead you to where you should sleep. What works for one won't work for another. I decided to paint one wall in my room and change the decor. Sleeping on a couch or a reclining chair is not the same as a bed. After about two years, it took a toll on my body. The Holy Spirit led me back to my bedroom. Actually, I think my body did!

Living the Good Life

*T*hough the journey has been rough, I've come out living a life that only God could have restored. I have overcome depression, rejection, and fear because of the Lord's restorative power. Just like Job, I've had so many things taken, stripped, and snatched away from me. In the past three years, I lost my remaining aunts and uncles and three cousins. I have watched my family disappear. Ben served so many roles in my life: husband, pastor, father of our children, cheerleader, sounding board, adviser, and designated driver (not because of alcohol but because I hate driving).

Just like Job, I have started gaining so many new abilities. He gave me back my joy, my inner peace, and a sound mind. He gave me confidence, and He removed my fear. I've regained full-time employment, earned another degree, written a testimony for widows, and found the ability to overcome the enemy's plot. I have reconnected with family members who I had lost connections with. I speak from pulpits and share my testimonies. Jesus spoke life into me, and I arose from the dead like Lazarus. I heard a pastor say some believed Jesus called Lazarus's name three times before he arose. *Well, it is the third year, and just look at me, God.* Let me pause right here to shout for a while.

Living the good life does not imply perfection or being rich in houses or land. It does not mean I am reclining on some theater-type couch. It means I am cognizant of what the Lord is doing for me and what He has already done. Furthermore, I am aware that my praise belongs to Him. He is worthy!

Forgive Me—I Was Wrong

Dear Diary,

We lash out at people in anger, frustration, and a multitude of other emotions. I did it, and I felt bad. It took me a few weeks, but I had to make a phone call to straighten it out. I had to apologize to a relative with good intentions and a well-meaning heart. When I did, I was relieved and freed. My uncle accepted my apology, and now I am like James Brown. I feel good.

Advice

We may not agree, but we are Christians first and foremost. When you are wrong, accept responsibility for it. Sweeping it under the rug or burying it in the sand will gnaw on your soul. Saying "I am sorry" or "I was wrong" are powerful and necessary parts of any apology. These words go a long way. When we wait a long time to apologize, it festers like an infected sore. It is never too late to apologize, of course, but the sooner it happens, the better. The best sermon we can give is the life we live.

We can talk reasonably without yelling and being disrespectful. We sometimes let our emotions take control. Keep calm—and know God is in control. Forgiveness is for the one who was wrong because it clears our conscience. We need to be strong enough to admit our faults and ask for forgiveness.

Oh, Happy Day

Dear Diary,

The children's book *Leo the Late Bloomer* was written by Robert Kraus. Leo was slower than his peers in walking, talking, and drawing. One day, in his own time, he bloomed. Just like Leo, I have bloomed! I am a happy lady. The analogy I like to use is that of a successful surgery. I went into the operation room, and the Great Physician has proclaimed that the surgery was a success. I have had my share of rehabilitation and recovery. I cannot describe the gratitude I have for the Lord. He healed me on every level: spiritually, emotionally, financially, and mentally. I walk with my head a bit higher. My smile is a bit wider. My steps are jaunty. My soul has been uplifted. I have been set free of depression and oppression. I have escaped bondage. It is a happy day.

Advice

It may not look or feel like it, but your happy day will come.

GRANDMA

Dear Diary,

I so miss my grandma during times like these. She would have some words of wisdom, a few laughs, and maybe some choice words. God has blessed me with my husband's grandma. She is kind but honest. When we talk, our conversations usually last for at least an hour. As Theodore Roosevelt would say, Ben's grandma speaks softly but carries a big stick. She has power behind her words. Her answer to most things is to respond with her favorite scripture (Philippians 4:13).

Advice

Maya Angelou said, "I've learned that people will forget what you said, people will forget what you did, but people will never forget how you made them feel." I have felt the sting and the blessing of this quote. I have been forgotten in some regards (sting), but I will never forget how people have made me feel (blessing).

MY PEOPLE

Enjoying "sister time" after Sunday
morning's worship. We are determined
to be lemonade makers for life.

Dear Diary,

Every frog praises its pond. I have some great people in
my family. I relish in the fact that they belong to me.
There are no trade-ins. This is the family God gave me,
and we accept each other for who we are. There are no
perfect people in my family, but many of us strive to
reach perfection to improve our lives. We lift each other
up and stand together for what is right. We celebrate

our successes and cry on each other's shoulders. We pass down life lessons to help the next generations. We don't all have the same relationship with God, but we are real, compassionate, and humanitarian.

Advice

In 1 Timothy 5:4, we see that a widow's children or nephews should show respect toward her. I believe this would be very helpful. However, family is united by more than DNA, adoption, or a marriage license. People who don't look like me or share the same ancestry could be family. The Word of God tells us that we will know we are his disciples by the love we have for one another (John 13:35). I have learned to not limit my mind to the definition of family. I've gained new family members along the way. I have family beyond the traditional mind-set. I have family at my church, at my workplace, in my neighborhood, and in my community. It is important to identity when Godliness is demonstrated toward you within your family. This is not to be taken for granted. Many people are not fortunate enough to have those types of relationships. It takes a village to raise a child (African proverb), but it takes a family to heal a widow. All family members can be defined as family due to logistics, but where matters of the heart are concerned, they may appear like strangers. Cherish your family—no matter who they are.

Dad, my siblings, and me.

My beautiful, precious mother.

My lovely sister.

My terrific trio.
From left to right: Mama, Grandma, and Aunt
Flossie (Aunt Sarah lovingly remembered).

Sunday morning with Dad.

My Christmas Present, 2015

Dear Diary,

My family just wanted me to heal. That very familiar question echoed throughout the Christmas season, especially from my girls. They asked, "What do you want for Christmas?"

I said, "Peace, love, and joy." Secretly, I asked the Lord for this and three other things that only God could provide: a clean heart, a renewed spirit, and a right mind. I cried out to Him in desperation. My back was against the wall. I felt helpless in my situation, but I knew just one touch from the Lord would remedy everything. He did it!

On Christmas morning at 11:54, my fourth grandchild was born.

My daughter whispered, "You got what you asked for."

I responded, "Peace, love, and joy—all wrapped together."

As time went on, God granted me the other three gifts. Only He could have done that. The dawn of a new day is beginning.

Advice

Just wait on it—He will give you the desires of your heart (Psalm 37:4).

Grandma's Christmas blessing!

The Power of Love

Dear Diary,

The Bible tells husbands to love their wives as Christ loves the church (Ephesians 5:25). Ben proclaimed his love for me in four weddings, which is quite phenomenal. We renewed our vows two weeks after we eloped and then on our nineteenth, twenty-fourth, and thirtieth anniversaries. Ben amazingly planned, coordinated, and orchestrated the latter three. Each time, he stood before family and friends and stated that he would let nothing but death separate us.

The minister repeatedly said, "You are no longer two but one."

Our finances were one, and our accomplishments were one. We had a spirit of singlemindedness and one heart. Today, I count it all joy (James 1:2–3) to experience such a blessing as this. Having a soul mate blessed me beyond measure. Having oneness allowed me to soar in my spirit and be wrapped in love.

Advice

I fully understand that there are no perfect marriages. I think of love as a rose garden. It is vibrant and smells so sweet, but roses have thorns that can be troublesome. Additionally, the flowers are fragile. Beauty does not come with the rose. If we do not nourish the plant, disease may befall upon it. Stephanie Mills sang, "I learn to respect the power of love." It is quite fine to still enjoy seeing couples in love, watching love stories, and looking at wedding dresses. They make me feel so happy.

Spiritual Awakening

*Y*ou are what you eat implies that your well-being is interwoven with your environment. Therefore, surround yourself with positivity. Better yet, become immersed in the Word of God. Watch Christian stations on cable and listen to gospel and Christian radio stations. Read Christian literature and study the Bible. The Word of God is your power source, your lifeline, and your sword. Everything you need is in the Word of God.

I was spiritually dead and not aware of who I was in God. The good part for me is that I became aware of this in the early stages of depression. Many people are dead and walking around unaware of their spiritual state. Everywhere I go, I see "dead" people. Yes! They are in a body, looking good with their designer suits, sew-ins, gel nails, and such. However, they are spiritually dead. On the outside, they are flawless, but on the inside, they are faulty.

Once you have risen, you are more aware of strongholds, demonic grips, and the like. Just knowing about them doesn't exempt one from the plots of Satan. We must apply the Word of God, believe it, and declare our victory. If I have the faith of a grain of a mustard seed I can move mountains (Matthew 17:20). I can tread on serpents and come out harmless (Luke 10:19). The spirit of God boldly tells us that we wrestle not with flesh and blood (Ephesians 6:12). It is not the person that is our problem—it is the demons within the person.

The Healing Place

Dear Diary,

Some commercials try to convince us that healing begins at a rehabilitation facility, which makes a valid point, but I beg to differ. Healing begins within the mind, heart, and soul. We are transformed by the renewing of our minds (Romans 12:2). Once our minds have been reformed, we will walk victoriously.

My first healing place was in my mind. I began to seek healing and desire living. I realized that I am not just here to take up space on God's green planet. I found a pastor and a church home that was ironically named "New Hope." My church firmly believes that there is no hopeless situation with God. Finally, I shifted job locations. It was totally divine intervention. I was hired at a school that sought teachers who would make a difference. After feeling almost worthless, I landed there. It was a rewarding experience to be among such fine individuals, and it was equally rewarding to know I was making a difference. I had a purpose again.

I had three healing places: my mind, my church, and my workplace. It all starts with the mind. Our school motto echoes in every classroom: "If I think I can, I can."

Advice

The United Negro College Fund proclaims, "The mind is a terrible thing to waste." You better believe it. Our minds control our destinies. It can hold us prisoner or set us free.

New Hope

Dear Diary,

After the passing of my husband, I decided it was proper to remain at my former church, which he pastored for twenty-one years, for at least one year. After all, I was the first lady emeritus, and I felt the need to remain loyal. We had three other ministers, and one delivered the message each week. It was different without Ben, but it felt familiar.

I knew my emotional condition required a shepherd. After a year, I asked the Lord to lead me to a new church home and a new pastor. After five months of searching, I still had no sign from God. I mentioned to a colleague that I was going to visit her church. She never asked me to visit, but she definitely stuck with me during my bereavement period. I went to my first worship service at New Hope, but nothing spoke to me about joining the congregation. However, my colleague invited me to their Hope Fest. Wow! An actual invitation—just for me. How special is that? I spoke to my handyman and postponed repairs to my house so I could attend the Hope Fest. The repairman's wife thought it sounded great and told her husband to go too. They had a transportation problem, but we worked to resolve the issue.

That was just prior to Thanksgiving in 2015. My heart was heavy because I had come to the startling conclusion that Ben was not my only loss. I had lost so many other things along the way. I meandered around the festival and noticed all the free items being given to the community. My previous church used to have giveaways too. Turkeys were being given away for Thanksgiving. It was exciting to see so many people being helped.

I noticed a familiar face in the crowd. Lo and behold, it was a former congregant of ours. While we talked, I heard a gospel song Ben used to sing. I was frozen in the crowd. I silently wept and then openly sobbed. Despite being comforted by our former church member, I felt alone in my sorrow. I could not compose myself. A kind woman asked if I was all right, and I told her I was not. I shared my story with her, and she guided me to a prayer table. While I was at the table, another kind woman prayed for me. The spirit of God within alerted me that I had found my church home. I informed her that I wanted to join their church right away. I introduced myself to the pastor and his lovely wife, and I found new hope at New Hope.

Advice

As humans, we want to remain in familiar places and maintain our traditions. Did you ever think that God was trying to take you away from familiar places or break traditions? Why would He want to do that? Maybe He wants to prove that a fish can actually live out of water if God moves it.

Celebrating my church's twenty-fifth anniversary.
Source: Lovely Lady Productions

Rosa and I met at work. We are colleagues,
Alpha Kappa Alpha sorority sisters (sorors), and
members of New Hope Baptist Church. Above
all Rosa has been a loyal friend on my journey.

THE LORD IS MY SHEPHERD

Dear Diary,

This has become up close and personal! The twenty-third psalm is probably the most popular psalm of all. Many people have memorized it in its entirety, and it is often recited in church. I was no different. This psalm was ritualistic, and I think I repeated it out of simple repetition. Other people may not be like me, but I did not truly live out the full meaning of the psalm until after Ben's death. Now, I hang onto every verse and every word in this familiar psalm.

The Lord is my shepherd; I shall not want (Psalm 23:1).

What was I thinking when I was trying to figure out how I was going to make it. I asked God for the Lotto numbers, and He told me I had already hit it. He said, "Look at how I keep blessing you." I did not believe God cared enough for me, but He did. He just kept making a way over and over again.

He maketh me lie down in green pastures: He leadeth me beside the still waters (Psalm 23:2).

I am able to rest due to the provisions given to me upon fertile ground. He waits until it is safe and guides me beside still waters. Then, He graciously allows me to move forward.

He restoreth my soul: He leadeth me in the paths of righteousness for His name's sake (Psalm 23:3).

He mended the broken pieces, and I appeared better and stronger than ever before. He assured me that doing right by Him was far more important than trying to please others—and He comforted my spirit.

Yea, though I walk through the valley of shadow of death, I will fear no evil, for thou art with me; thy rod and thy staff, they comfort me (Psalm 23:4). I do not have to worry about evildoers because when the viper attached to Paul, no medical ill befell him (Acts 28:5).

I can take comfort in knowing He is in control. I do not fear death. I can lean on God to comfort, guide, and protect me.

Thou preparest a table before me in the presence of mine enemies: thou anointest my head with oil; my cup runneth over (Psalm 23:5).

To prove He was God, He showed my blessings to others in case there were some doubting Thomases. He blessed me through my job and by furthering my education, acquiring a support team to heal, restoring my health, and giving me a right mind.

Surely goodness and mercy shall follow me all the days of my life; and I will dwell in the house of the Lord forever (Psalm 23:6).

His blessings and mercy will last me from here to eternity. I must continue to live for Him and know that He is able to do anything but fail.

Advice

When you get closer to God, you will be enlightened. The scriptures will develop a closer and more personal meaning for you.

LEVELS OF CHRISTIANITY

Dear Diary,

I always hear Christians saying that God is bringing us up to a new level. I thought my level must look pretty pitiful at times, and I decided to come up with my own levels. Each level carries the previous level's qualities and builds upon the others.

Levels of Christianity

Level 1: Repent and believe in Jesus (Mark 1:15). Remember the thief on the cross.

Level 2: Repent, believe, and be baptized (Romans, 10:9, Acts 2:38).

Level 3: Become a follower of Jesus and serve others (Matthew 25:40–45).

Level 4: Pray without ceasing (1 Thessalonians 5:17).

Level 5: In all things, give thanks (1 Thessalonians 5:18).

Level 6: Love your enemies, bless them that curse you, do good to them that hate you, and pray for them which despitefully use you and persecute you (Matthew 5:44).

Level 7: Assemble together with your sisters and brothers (Hebrews 10:25).

Level 8: Study the Word of God, read the Bible, attend Bible study and/or Sunday school (2 Timothy 2:15).

Level 9: Share your testimonies with other individuals (Luke 22:32).

Level 10: Engage in spiritual warfare by exercising the power to tread on serpents (Luke 10:19). Wait until your change comes (Job 14:14). Encourage yourself in the Lord (1 Samuel 30:6). Don't be weary in well doing for you shall reap if you faint not (Galatians 6:9).

Advice

The levels are always changing. Just because I sometimes scored a 10 did not mean I had arrived. We are all works in progress. Back in the day, a "ten" was a lady's "brick-house" figure of 36-24-36, but our shapes changed. One day, I went to work on level 10. Then, one phone call threw me down to a level 3. Another day, a driver behind me was ranting and raving. I dropped again. We have all sinned and fallen short in the past tense (Romans 3:23). We are constantly sinning in the present tense— whether in our thoughts or actions. Nevertheless, we get back in the race and keep working again.

My Last Will and Testament

Dear Diary,

I have an actual last will and testament completed by my attorney. I know there is much more to me than that. I am inspired by Mary McLeod Bethune's *Last Will and Testament*. It leaves more than earthly possessions. There is much more to me than church suits, hats, porcelain dolls, angels, and collectibles. There are some things my children and grandchildren should know I have left them. Their job is to continuously pass the baton.

My Last Will and Testament

I leave you a commitment to God that includes worshipping Him in the sanctuary to which you belong (Hebrews 10:25), serving others (Matthew 25:40), and giving Him a portion of your earnings (Proverbs 3:9–10).

I leave you a spirit of love that should be put into action with family members and others—regardless of wealth, education, or immoral living. Love conquers all (1 Corinthians 13:4–8) and can manifest itself tenderly or sternly.

I leave you wisdom, which is obtained through God, notable others, and life experiences. It is godly living, common sense, and wit combined into one product.

I leave you servitude, which is more of a blessing for the server than the one being served. It makes your heart sing, and the Lord smiles upon you.

I leave you respect toward others. If you respect yourself first and foremost, it will be easier to respect others. Hence, it will thrust others to respect you. Ultimately, respect will make or break you in the real world.

I leave you a family; in each life I have touched, there is a piece of me. Find that piece and know whatsoever is lovely, whatsoever is pure, and think on these things (Philippians 4:8–11).

I leave you a yearning for education because it is power. Life is more comfortable with it than without it. This includes a formal education, spiritual education, and financial education.

I leave you with a strong work ethic because faith without works is dead (James 2:14–26). The Bible tells us if a man does not work, he should not eat (2 Thessalonians 3:10).

I leave you a sense of responsibility because it will ensure that the job is performed decently, to the best of one's ability, and with satisfaction. Being responsible holds me responsible and minimizes blaming others.

Advice

Of course, these are my greatest attributes. Ben and I laid this foundation for our children and others to follow. Every person should leave behind a legacy. I suggest writing down what you leave behind because it helps define your purpose.

At the End of the Day

Dear Diary,

I have often heard the expression "at the end of the day." Its underlying theme speaks to what matters most. At the end of the day, my feelings do not matter. I might have been called some names, been treated unkindly, or even been on the uninvited list, but it does not matter because the Lord wanted me to draw closer to Him. It was never about people. It was about Jesus. It was about my journey and having the stamina to endure spiritual warfare. It was about being a female Job. It was about overcoming losses and the Lord blessing me with gains. Nothing else matters. Paul refers to his past trials as dung (Philippians 3:8). Now is the time to forget the things behind me (Philippians 3:13) and press on to a higher calling.

What matters is that I am healed from depression, oppression, and rejection. I know who I am and who I belong to. I have a purpose, and it is not just to take up space on God's green planet. After asking God about my mission, He allowed me to find the answer in the trunk of my husband's car. There was a poster with the words of Dr. Martin Luther King Jr.: "Life's most urgent and persistent question is, what have you done to serve others?" I was stripped of the title of wife and pastor's wife for His glory. He wanted me to acknowledge that, at the end of the day, I am His servant. My mission is to encourage the discouraged, bring joy to the bereaved, give hope to the hopeless, and include the rejected. For we are cautioned in Matthew 25:40 that, whatsoever we have done to the least one, we have done it unto Him. Just like Job, at the end of the day, I got it back! Thank You, Jesus. I've got the victory!

Advice

Once you are spiritually awakened, it is just like the old Negro spiritual "When the Morning Comes." You will understand it better by and by.

Mourning to Morning

Dear Diary,

Hello, my name is Toni Adams. I am healed by the power of God. I am no longer that sad person who is overcome with grief. Being rejected no longer has a stronghold over me. I have gone from the valley of mourning to the mountaintop of morning. I have reached the point in my life where I have personally witnessed that "weeping endureth for a night, but joy come in the morning" (Psalm 30:5). It is a glorious morning and a brand-new day. The birds are chirping. The dew is still on the roses. The vibrant sunshine radiates warmth upon my face. It is the official beginning of a new spiritual workday. Goodbye, mourning—and hello, morning.

Advice

Your beginning does not have to master your ending. What God has done for others, He can do for you. Always know that you are here for a reason. Ask God to reveal your purpose. After you have been strengthened, go forth and strengthen others (Luke 22:31–34). Dr. Maya Angelou's "On the Pulse of Morning" offers some optimistic advice for those who have lived through the challenges of life: "When you have preserved and conquered, say simply, very simply, with hope, "Good morning."

SUMMARY: A CHRISTIAN'S RESPONSIBILITY

The book of James tells us to take care of widows and orphans. Who does that anymore? You are grieving and overcome with many emotions. You must take care of yourself. I promise you that, after the funeral, you will be forgotten by many people, including those who supposedly were close to you. Here are a few words of advice:

- Take action toward your healing. Upon my sister's advice, I enrolled in Grief Share. This is a thirteen-week program to help you deal with grief in a Christian way. Grief Share recommends DEER as a remedy to recover: drink, eat, exercise, and rest. This will aid you in living.
- After the funeral, visit a doctor. Grief affects the mind, body, and spirit. Depression can hide and reveal itself in many forms.
- If you are not hungry, train yourself to eat mechanically, which means eating at certain times of the day. Eat fewer processed foods to become healthier.
- Don't be afraid to visit a psychologist. Psychologists are good sounding boards and allow you to see

problems from another perspective. Plus, they are obligated to keep your personal life confidential.

- Locate support groups for widows. It is a blessing when you can relate to someone who is experiencing the same crisis.
- Allocate time for prayer or meditation. It helps to talk to God or simply think on good things (Philippians 4:8).
- Surround yourself with positive people, places, and things.
- Take care of your needs and put your wants aside.
- Know your limits. My stressful teaching job required high functionality, decision-making, and intense concentration. Upon the doctor's recommendation, I took time to heal and digest what had happened since Ben's sudden death. I took two leaves of absence due to depression. Later, I accepted a job that was less intense.
- Embrace new friendships. People are seasonal. God will give you what you need through each season.
- Save your money for what-if situations: job loss, ill health, and returning children and grandchildren. Avoid creating more bills, making major purchases, and loaning large amounts of money.

- Know that some people will gravitate to you because they believe you just won the Lotto, and others will shun you because they feel you are poor and needy.
- Relieve your stress through exercise, reading, listening to sermons or inspirational messages, or even lighting a candle.

Resources for Widows

- American Widow Project (for widows with military husbands) http://americanwidowproject.org/
- Grief Share (bereavement and loss) https://www.griefshare.org/
- Liz Logelin Foundation (widows/widowers with young families) http://thelizlogelinfoundation.org/
- Open to Hope (death, grief and loss) www.opentohope.com/
- Sisterhood of Widows (grief support) http://sisterhoodofwidows.com/
- Soaring Spirits International (support in widowhood) www.soaringspirits.org
- W Connection (resources) http://www.wconnection.org
- Widows of Hope (resources for widows/widowers) www.widowshope.org/
- Widows and Widowers Support Group (social support) https://www.meetup.com/topics/widows-and-widowers-support-group/
- Widow's Well (financial matters) http://www.churchinvestorsfund.org/widows-well-statisticss

Special Days for Widows

May 3, 2017, was the first annual National Widow's Day. The day, inspired by Widow Wednesday, encourages people to show acts of kindness toward widows on that particular Wednesday and on future Wednesdays.

June 23 is International Widow's Day. The day is set aside to give attention to widows in regard to poverty and injustice. Widows in other countries are often ostracized and discriminated. Therefore, the author A. Anhalt stresses the importance of widows sharing their stories to heighten awareness of this sector of our population.

Facts about Widows

- The pain of widowhood lasts more than one year.
- A grieving widow who lives alone may not hear another voice for days.
- A grieving widow's pain is unique.
- Grieving widows are often physically and emotionally fatigued.
- A grieving widow adores her children.
- A grieving widow often feels like an afterthought.
- A grieving widow can be a gift to others.
- A grieving widow's finances will take a drastic change.
- God has compassion for widows.

Reference: Gaye Clark, The Gospel Coalition, 2015

Scriptural Mentions of Widows

- We are cautioned to care for widows (James 1:27).
- Using a widow is not advisable (Exodus 22:22–24).
- Blessing a widow will result in being blessed (Deuteronomy 14:29).
- God hears the prayers of a widow (Exodus 22:23).
- God has a purpose for widows (Jeremiah 29:11).

Reference: Anna Gate, 2014

Statistics about Widows

- In 2011, the US Census Bureau reported that the median age of widowhood across all ethnicities was 59.4 for a first marriage and 60.3 for a second marriage (Amy Florian, 2013).
- The average widow will be on her own for fourteen years (Widow's Well 2014).
- Widowhood is associated with acquiring new roles, financial distress, and changes in relationships, which affects psychological well-being. (Sasson and Umberson 2013)

TV Shows and Movies about Widows/Widowers

As a child, I recall a few TV shows that starred characters that were widowers: *Courtship of Eddie's Father, Andy Griffith, Sanford and Son, and My Three Sons*. TV shows during my childhood that starred widows included *Good Times, The Partridge Family, and Golden Girls*.

Movies about widowhood can trigger many emotions. Depending on the cause of death of the spouse, where we are in the healing process, and if we elect to watch the movie on a special day, the result can be helpful or hurtful. This list of widow-themed movies is designed to increase awareness. The genres include comedy, drama, mystery, romance, and documentary.

- *Beyond Belief* (2007)
- *Contagion* (2011)
- *Dan in Real Time* (2007)
- *Dragonfly* (2002)
- *Finding Jenua* (2011)
- *Love's Everlasting Courage* (2011)
- *Love Happens* (2009)
- *P.S. I Love You* (2007)
- *Smart People* (2008)
- *The American President* (1995)
- *The Boys are Back* (2009)
- *The Descendants* (2011)
- *The Iron Lady* (2012)
- *The Widow's Might* (2009)
- *Three Colours: Blue* (1993)
- *Truly, Madly, Deeply* (1990)
- *Water* (2005)
- *We Bought a Zoo* (2011)
- *Weeds* (2005)
- *What a Way to Go!* (1964)
- *Widows* (2018)
- *Yours, Mine, and Ours* (2006)

Famous Young Widows/Widowers

- Faith Evans (21)
- Jean Harlow (21)
- Martha Washington (25)
- Elizabeth Taylor (26)
- Theodore Roosevelt (26)
- Anna Nicole Smith (28)
- Ralph Waldo Emerson (29)
- Joe Biden (30)
- Myrlie Evers-Williams (30)
- Betty Shabazz (30)
- Jackie Kennedy Onassis (34)
- Pierce Brosnan (38)
- Katie Couric (41)
- Coretta Scott King (41)
- Bo Derek (41)
- Terri Irwin (42)
- Henry Fonda (45)
- Celine Dion (48)

WAYS TO HELP WIDOWS

- Provide a meal for them.
- Watch their children.
- Perform or pay for housekeeping needs.
- Buy gifts for a special occasion.
- Become a positive role model for their children.
- Send them an invitation.
- Repair something for them.
- Complete a chore for a widow while you do your own.
- Talk with them.

Reference: On Faith (2015)

SEVEN WAYS CHURCHES CAN SHOW THEY CARE ABOUT WIDOWS

- Stay in contact with them.
- Express sympathy for their loss.
- Avoid saying, "Call me if you need me." Instead, ask for specific errands that might need to be done.
- Do not avoid conversations about the widow's husband.
- Invite a widow to something.
- Encourage the widow that this season will pass.
- Fulfill your promises to widows.
- (Crosswalk)

Reference: reference source.Crosswalk.com

References

Angelou, Maya. "On the Pulse of the Morning." Retrieved from https://www.youtube.com/watch?v=59xGmHzxtZ4.

Angelou, Maya. Brainy quotes. Retrieved from https://www.brainyquote.com/quotes/authors/m/maya_angelou.html.

Anhalt, A. 2017 Mission Network News Protecting the Invisible on International Widows' Day. Retrieved from https://www.mnnonline.org/news/protecting-invisible-international-widows-day/.

Bachararach, B., and C. Bayer-Sayer. 1993. "Anniversary Lyrics." Accessed September 14, 2017. https://www.lyrics.com/lyric/6540253.

Bradley, W., Jr. 2017. New Hope Baptist Church.

Clark, G. 2015. 9 things you need to know about widows. The Gospel Coalition. Retrieved from https://www.thegospelcoalition.org/article/9-things-you-need-to-know-about-widows.

Crosswalk.com. Seven Ways You Can Help Widows in Your Church. Retrieved from http://www.crosswalk.com/church/pastors-or-leadership/7-ways-you-can-help-widows-in-your-church.html.

Florian, A. 2013. Serving widowed clients whatever their age. Retrieved from http://www.fa-mag.com/news/serving-widowed-clients-whatever-their-age-14829.html.

Gamble, K., L. Huff, and A. Jackson. 1973. Lyrics.com, STANDS4 LLC, 2017. "For the Love of Money Lyrics." Accessed September 14, 2017. https://www.lyrics.com/lyric/5088522.

Gate, A. 2014. Facts about widows. Retrieved from https://annasgate.org/facts-widows/.

Grief Share. Your journey from mourning to joy. 2007.

Holy Bible. Retrieved from https://www.Biblegateway.com.

Hughes, L. 1922. "Mother to Son."

King, M. L., Jr. Brainy quotes. Retrieved from https://www.brainyquote.com/quotes/authors/m/martin_luther_king_jr.html.

Kraus, Robert. 1971. *Leo the Late Bloomer.*

On Faith. 2015. Ten ways to Care for Widows and Orphans. Retrieved from https://www.onfaith.co/onfaith/2015/01/19/10-ways-to-care-for-widows-and-orphans/35894.

Perren, F., F. Mizell, D. Richards, and B. Gordy. 1970. ABC. Retrieved from http://www.songfacts.com/detail.php?id=1830.

Rodger, R., and O. Hammerstein. "Getting to Know You."

Sasson, I., and D. J. Umberson 2013. Widowhood and Depression: New Light on Gender Differences, Selection, and Psychological Adjustment. Retrieved from https://academic.oup.com/psychsocgerontology/article/69B/1/135/542138/Widowhood-and-Depression-New-Light-on-Gender.

Stevenson, M. 1939. Footprints in the Sand. Retrieved from http://www.footprints-inthe-sand.com/.

Louisiana Weekly. 2014. Police shootings of Unarmed Black Men a National Problem. Retrieved from http://www.louisianaweekly.com/police-shootings-of-unarmed-black-men-a-national-problem/.

Widow Wednesday. 2014. May 3 National Widow's Day, Retrieved from http://widowwednesday.com/national-widows-day/.

Widow's Well. Retrieved from http://www.churchinvestorsfund.org/widows-well-statisticss.

Winbash, A., and R. Moore. 1985. "I Have Learned to Respect the Power of Love Lyrics." Accessed September 14, 2017. https://www.lyrics.com/lyric/5021719.